From Correctional Officer to
Youth Counselor

My struggle to help others, and myself.

ISBN 978-1470088835

My story is dedicated to the men and women who continue to fight the good fight, throughout this country, to help the lives of others.

But does it come with benefits?

I remember it like it was yesterday. It was Spring of 2000. I had just graduated from college, and I did what most up and coming graduates did after graduation for the first few months. I did absolutely nothing. I stayed away from anything that resembled books, learning, and any form of gathering knowledge. I figured, if I was going to learn anything else from this point on, it would be to make me money. In my own mind, I was destined for greatness. I had such high expectations for myself. I planned on working for some big company, and earning lots of income. However, my degree was in Criminal Justice. Which obviously made no sense, but I enjoyed the courses they offered. Well, turns out, you shouldn't major in something because you can take a class called 'Organized Crime and Drugs' as part of the curriculum.

I even remember graduation day. I told my fellow Criminal Justice majors exactly what I would do with this degree. I told everyone I was going to wipe my butt with it, and get a real job in a real field of work. To be honest, I did end up doing something completely different in the end, so I was right. I just wasn't expecting the difference to be so great, or so emotionally draining, or so rewarding at the same time.

So there I was, still living in my parents' house, with a degree in something I had no use for. That is, until my father had this brilliant idea.

"Hey, son, you need a job with benefits. Do you
know what it means to have a job with great benefits?"
"Uh, no".
"Well you can't just sit around all day like a bum, so I
think you should join law enforcement"
"Well, dad, I don't feel like getting shot at"
"So then you will work in the jail, the benefits are just
as great".

And so there I was, a couple weeks later, in my most
ridiculous outfit of an old t-shirt, cargo shorts and flip flops,
being woken up at 7 in the morning so that I can be driven
by my father to jail. Ok, it was an office room in the building
of the jail, but what's the difference, really.

It was there that I found myself once again taking an
exam, only this time, passing the exam means I go straight to
jail, so to speak. Oh, I guess this is the part of the story
where I am supposed to admit that I somehow managed to
fail that basic skills reading and math test that day, and had
to retake it later to pass, but what college graduate would
admit that and publish it for all to read. Anyway, I spent
the next few months of my life in boot camp, being yelled at,
ridiculed, put down, and given more tests. All the while
thinking the same thing over and over. "What was I doing
here? I don't even like law enforcement. I don't even like
cops. Well, except for my dad that is. I learned a lot about
myself during this time, and I will always remember the
accomplishment and achievement of going through such an
experience successfully. However, I will also never forget
what that achievement awarded me. So on to jail I went to
start my career profession. Don't pass go, collect a
paycheck.

Ok, well, I guess it's time I finally learned about the
world of 'benefits'. Did you know that if you were to spend
the next 20 to 30 years of your life going to jail eight hours

per day, you would receive lots of free medical check-ups, dental cleanings, and a nice amount of vacation and sick time. But who would want to use those days and ever avoid going to jail for a day? And you get to own a gun. How about that for benefits? Oh, and ladies and gentlemen, that's not all. When you become an old man/woman, after having spent most of your adult life surrounded by criminals, you will now live out your last few years receiving another check in the mail, in addition to social security. That's right. The all important, all mighty, 'Pension Plan'. That certainly makes it all worth it, right dad? Now, of course, there are obviously huge benefits to having such financial stability during your retirement age. My father has certainly been reaping the benefits for years now. But my father always loved what he did. He took pride in his uniform. He took pride in his service to society. Whether it was as a police officer in the NYPD in New York, or as a correctional officer in a county jail in the state of Florida, he always knew what was best. Not only what was best for him, but more importantly, what was best for his family.

So I gave it a shot. I did the best I could. I put in my time and worked my hours. Or, as my dad would always say, "eight and hit the gate". Meaning, work your eight hours and then head straight for the exit. Forget everything that just happened during the past eight hours. Head straight home, take off the uniform, relax, and immediately put your mind back to reality. This is something I tried to learn early on in my career. The concept of separating work from home. This is something, 10 years later, I have still yet to perfect.

I have to admit, I learned a lot while working in this environment. I learned about the darker side of society. I learned about a man's struggle to survive. I learned about what it is like to see someone on their worst possible day.

And I watched as many of them went through it over and over again, like the movie groundhog day. I learned about the idea of listening, the art of patience, and the power of observation. Tools I continue to have, utilize, and benefit from to this day.

Early on in my career, I met a 21 year old inmate who already had two children, ages 5 and 6. The mother of his children had their first when she was 14. So how did they manage? Well, for him, he did what he thought was right. He stole his way to financial security. He even told me stories about actually using his children to steal while out in the community. He had so many stories to tell. So many stories of cons, accomplishments, and failures. The one thing I don't remember hearing too much about was his children. What were the children doing? Were they safe? What kind of future do they have ahead of them? What will become of them? What will become of him? And why should I even care? Maybe it was the start of something for me. Maybe it was something in me.

I also briefly met a teenager, who, at the time had become famous, or shall I say, infamous. He was the kid who shot and killed his teacher. It was all over the local and national news at the time. What fascinated me the most about this kid was his personality. He seemed happy and content, laughing and playing in the unit with the others. Like any other 14 year old, I found myself telling the kid to 'slow down', 'stop running', 'quite down'. He didn't seem to have a care in the world. I never understood that. While seeing this young man go about his day, and hearing all the stories from the 21 year old about his 'adventures in thievery', I never once saw them show regret. Show remorse. Show some sense of disappointment in their eyes for what they have become. Maybe it was their way of coping with the situation. Maybe it was their only way of keeping their sanity, keeping their faith, and holding on to hope for a better tomorrow. Or maybe they were just trying to get through each day.

I felt like maybe I would never see such a thing in jail regarding remorse, until I worked one night in the lockdown unit. It's the part of the jail where inmates remain in their cell for 23 of the 24 hours a day. This one night, I met a 17 year old young man. All he had in his cell were clothes, a pencil, paper, and a bible. Throughout that eight hour shift, I talked with that young man about his situation. He told me about his bad decisions, his bad choices, and the willingness to change his life, go in another direction, and not just be a statistic. It was during this conversation that I thought about his family. Where were his parents? Where were his teachers? Where were his role models? At times, I wondered why I was even talking to him at all. My job was to observe and report, not listen and counsel.

I had a long talk with him that night, sharing my thoughts with him, sharing my well wishes, and offering my blessings and hope for a better future for him. But I was meeting him in jail. This was no scared straight program. There was no police officer visiting his classroom teaching him the rights and wrongs of society. And there was no going home to reflect on what was taught and make a new conscious decision on what road to take next.

From that point on, I started wondering what I was doing there. I had a good job, a good profession, with 'benefits', but what was I accomplishing? What was I truly achieving in life? And what good was I to others in this capacity? I distinctly remember the looks on my fellow officer's faces every day at work. Just from the body language of my coworkers, I could tell whether it was their first day of the five day work week, or their last. It was the looks of the ones on their 'Monday' that always troubled me.

As a child, I always imagined myself being rich. I imagined myself accomplishing all my dreams. I imagined myself being happy. I never imagined that, as an adult, I would be just another guy who has the 'it's my Monday' look on my face. Perhaps I was meant for something different. Perhaps I was meant to help others, and not just monitor them.

Well, let's just say that my career profession in law enforcement didn't last long. Amazingly enough, I felt as though being surrounded by inmates, in an enclosed room with no fresh air coming in, for the rest of my adult life may not truly fulfill whatever dreams, goals, and plans I may have had for myself. So alas, I soon said farewell to the land of 'Pension Plan', I mean, the land of law enforcement, to explore a new way of life.

So, what to do? My only full-time job experience was in wearing a uniform, and telling grown men to make their bed. So, I did what everyone does in this country, I got a hook-up from a friend with a job. I was told that, by simply being male, I could easily get a job working as a case manager for a social service agency. Apparently, there are not many males working in the field. So, I faxed off my resume, hoped they would notice my name looked male, and tried not to blow the interview. And then, without really thinking the whole thing through, I got what I asked for. I got a chance to work with children. I started working in the interesting world of social services, AKA 'non-profit.'

Non-Profit

The term Non-Profit has always fascinated me. I
mean, they make it sound like nobody makes money. Well,
pretty much every single non-profit agency director I ever
met seemed to have more money than God. At least,
compared to what I was making anyway. Am I the only one
working in this field that saw the bosses roll up in a
BMW/Mercedes/Lexus every morning? But, what the heck,
it's a job working with children. Children who still have a
chance. Children who are not already in a jail cell, on 24
hour lockdown, living with regret for what might have been.
This kind of job should give me purpose, right? How bad
can that be? Oh, and it also comes with benefits.
I've always heard about nonprofit growing up. To
me, it was perceived as this great gift from a society of pain.
To me, nonprofit meant that, throughout the country, there
were agencies devoted to changing the lives of others. I
thought about it in terms of those heart wrenching
commercials/infomercials about starving children in Africa,
or health clinics for children without insurance. This is
where I felt I could make a difference. I used the mentality
of ,'somebody has to do it, so why not me'?
When one thinks of nonprofit, one thinks of a group
of caring individuals, banding together, to help right the
wrongs of society. Help fix what is broken. Help heal what
is pained. And give hope to those who feel lost. However,
what I learned very early on, is that nonprofit has nothing to
do with lack of riches. It's just that I was in the group of
those who never see a piece of it. In the end, I believe I still
got what I was looking for. I still became that in which I
perceived to be a part of. I became a part of my own band of
brothers/sisters in arms. I felt like I was becoming my own
version of the starving children infomercials. I guess I just

didn't realize how much profit others were to gain off of my work. I never truly realized the resentment I would begin to carry knowing this fact. I never realized the effects it could have on the one's I am to be helping. From the beginning of my work in nonprofit, I started to feel like I was back in jail again. Only, instead of taking a 'don't want to go to jail' sick day from work, I now started taking the 'mental health' day off.

Growing up, I really never understood the term 'mental health' day. My dad, who wore a uniform practically his entire adult life, never really took a day off. You take a day off when you're sick. And you better be really sick, because you don't want to inconvenience your fellow brothers/sisters in arms in finding someone to cover for you when you're out. Plus, up to this point in my life, I had only worked part time jobs outside of time working in the jail. Jobs in which I needed to work every one of those days to get paid. I ended up taking a lot of days off from work at the jail. It wasn't that I was really sick. And it wasn't that I did not respect my co-workers. It was that I would continually be drained, not psychically, but mentally. I guess I thought that if I did something I felt was more meaningful, I would no longer have those feelings. Well, I guess not everything is what it seems.

I've always loved my mental health days in social services. It's that time of year, well, ok, that time every month, where you give yourself a much deserved, or at least earned based on your benefits package, day off from work.

Americans, throughout the world, are known for working the longest hours, most amounts of days, and highest desire to earn every penny possible. The field of social services, and its employees, are no exception, except for the making more money part. I would often find myself heading out to a child's house at 7 am to drive them to school. And then later on leaving a family's home at 7pm, only to get a call from another parent frantically worried about her son, causing me to be on the phone for another hour or so.

Usually, when I took my day off from law enforcement, I would find myself sleeping in, relaxing, and watching TV. In the field of social services, I usually would find myself lying awake all night the night before, thinking about how great it's going to be to call out sick. Only to awake in the morning, make the phone call, and then spend the next hour or so wondering if anything bad will happen with one of the children. To then go in the next morning, and learn about crisis A, drama B, chaos C that is coming my way for the rest of the week. What is the 'benefit' in that?

It could definitely be overwhelming at times. It's supposed to just be a job. Just a way to pay the bills. But remember, I saw this as an opportunity to have purpose. Maybe that is where I went wrong. I started to make it about me. I started to make it about my needs, my wants, and my desires. It's amazing how a person can be so giving, yet so needy at the same time. I've always had so many dreams for myself, and began to work hard to help make dreams happen for others. However, at the same time, I guess I always felt as though I should somehow be further rewarded for the accomplishments of others. A life of purpose meant of life of happiness. And a life of happiness, to me, always involved money.

To this day, 10 years later, I will never truly understand why I have never moved on to another field of work. I paid my dues. I did my good deed for society. Yet here I am, year after year, job after job, and agency after agency, still putting in the good fight. Still fighting with management, still complaining over money, and still wanting more financial stability. And I will tell you this. I will never regret one minute of it.

Get paid to learn

One of my heroes in life, Mark Cuban, was quoted in one of his books, basically stating that, instead of just furthering your education through school, why not get paid to learn. And that is what I felt I have been doing. I have been learning. Each and every day of my life, I am educated by others. And though I am not learning in the business world, I am learning something that is possibly far more important. I am learning about what I perceive to be the hardest business of all. The business of children and family. The business of life.

You just can't buy the type of education I have received during this time. It is not every day that someone with a college degree in criminal justice, is sitting in a court room, advocating for a young man facing 3 years in a youth camp, and spending a good part of the next 2 years of your 'work life' making sure that doesn't happen by providing hands on, in-home support to that child and family. But that's a story for later in this book. For now, let's focus on the task at hand. The task of tackling the world of life and work in non-profit, and learning as I go.

People say it all the time. You have to separate your work life from your home life. This makes all the sense in the world to me. I never really did a great job of it working in the jail, but I began to get better at it towards the end. But what if your work life involves listening, day in, day out, to stories of hardship, failure, triumph, discrimination and hate? Not from people with criminal records but from children, parents, and grandparents struggling just to stay above water in life. I guess it would be easy for me to go to work, travel around the city, counsel youth and families on the values of sharing, strength, confidence and success, only to later go home to my own apartment, watch my nice TV, count on my parents to always be there if I need them, and use my credit card to purchase any needed emergency items if personal disaster strikes.

But what if your parents are not there for you? What if you don't have credit cards to bail yourself out? What if your voice was not being heard? Voice. This is something that should be the cornerstone of anything and everything I write about pertaining to children, families, and the business of social services. What are we without our voice? What are we without our vision? What we become is that without purpose. And one without purpose is one without hope. And without hope…

I found myself, day after day, week after week, year after year, helping others find their hope. Hope in the form of therapy. Hope in the form of tutoring. Hope in the form of sports activities. I have spent most of my adult life, not wearing a uniform like my dad, but bearing the weight of other's frustrations, hardship, and hope. It is that weight that has seemed to be my downfall, in my own mind, all these years. It's the lives of others that became my life. It were their responsibilities that became my responsibilities. It was their hope that became mine. I took on these challenges from the very beginning of my career, and continued to do so for a long time to come.

The start of my journey into non profit

My first job in non-profit was as a case manager in the state of Florida. Well, that sounds simple enough. Talk with some families, ask what they need, and help them get it. Simple, straight forward. Yeah, well, I knew it was no longer 'straight forward' as soon as the first single-mother came to me on a Friday and said, "So here's the deal. Is there any way I can get rent money from you guys, because if I don't get it by end of today, my son and I will probably spend the weekend packing up our stuff, sneaking out in the middle of the night, and heading to a shelter". And that is what I consider my initiation into non-profit.

This initiation felt like the combination of hell week in a fraternity, and being jumped into a gang, all into one eight hour day. It all starts, as everything should, in the beginning. I, of course, went directly to my supervisor.

Me: "Hey Dawn, (that's boss's name. I never called anyone boss, supervisor, anything that would show I considered them a form of authority, because I seem to have a problem with that), this Child's mother needs money".
Dawn: "When does she need it by"?
Me: "Yesterday" (yeah, even during times of stress, I'm sarcastic)
Dawn: "Well, I think we have it in the budget, but the director is currently on vacation, and she is the only one who can sign the check"
Me: "Are you kidding me?"
Dawn: "You can try calling the assistant director and ask what steps we can take"

So I called the assistant director:

Me: "Yeah, Hi Martha, I need your help, a parent needs emergency rent money to keep from being evicted by end of today"
Martha: "Well, unfortunately, Susan is on vacation, and is currently out overseeing the opening of her new restaurant". Oh yeah, that's not a misprint, the Director, who never worked a day in her life in the field of social services, was opening up a high end restaurant in a fancy neighborhood she lived in.
Me: "What the......well can't you sign it?"
Martha: "No, I cannot sign it, and I don't like the way your speaking to me right now".
Me: " Ok, sorry, but can we figure something out, because they really need the money".
Martha: "You have to understand how things work here, you can't just speak to me like this, there is a way to go about things.....blah blah blah.....blah blah blah........"

I kind of zoned out the rest of the conversation, and eventually hung up on her.....yeah, I know, but like I said, not good with authority, especially when I think they are idiots.

Anyway, not shockingly enough, my 'supervisor' Dawn took me aside about 30 minutes later, asked me why I was so disrespectful towards Martha, and stated that the Director was nice enough to sign the physical check for the money, as long as I was willing and able to drive to her restaurant and hand deliver it to her.

So, I did what I had to do. I went to the restaurant, got her to sign the check and was on my way. Of course, I had to first listen to this lady inform me that the restaurant should be open by end of the month, and that I should come by some time and try it out. Yeah, Like I could afford anything on the menu. My car alone would be an embarrassment to the parking lot of the place. So I took off and headed across the other side of town to meet with the family. The end result was that mom got the money. No sneaking out middle of the night. Problem eventually solved. Emotional rollercoaster officially ends...for now.

If that was my initiation into nonprofit work, I think my first call of duty really came before that when, during my first two weeks on the job, I learned something very important about nonprofit. I learned that.....well.....you are not going to learn anything from anyone......meaning......you are pretty much on your own to learn how to do your job.

It's like your mom or dad sitting down with you at age 16, teaching you only how to open the car door and turn the ignition with the key, and then telling you to hop in and go for a ride. And that is exactly what I felt like I have been doing for ten years. One wild ride. In my eyes, it was inevitably up to me to succeed and fail through trial and error. It was up to me to 'learn as I go', learn from my mistakes, and figure out what works best for each individual. The down side, obviously, is that it's the children and their families who have to suffer a little with me. It's their lives I am learning from. It's their futures in the balance. My mistakes would cause me some mental hardship, but cause these families so much more.

Sure, like most jobs, there are always 'training' classes/courses. But you never actually learned anything pertinent to your day to day work. What I learned, in this case, is that these trainings mostly ended up always being a venting-fest for staff. It was that time of the week, when, while not being surrounded by family chaos, staff vented about their frustrations, their crisis situations, their feelings, and hopes for improvement with management. At first, I fell into the drama as well. I always found myself being front and center in stating my frustrations, and being brutally honest in doing so. But, in the end, the only thing I really learned was that, by doing this, all I did was make the so-called training last longer than it should have. So I quickly learned to stay silent, and hope to get out early.

It was also during this first non-profit employment that I learned all about the wonderful world of auditing. You see, while the banking industry is a mess, the mortgage lending industry is a mess, and honestly, the government is a mess, the one thing that Non-profit apparently takes some form of priority on is the idea of constant and overwhelming oversee and monitoring of your every move.

What a wonderful idea. Of course I did not have enough on my plate when it came to helping children and families pay rent, receive counseling, stay in school, and stay out of juvenile hall. I also had to spend at least one full week every 6-12 months re-reading and reviewing everything I ever documented, gathered, obtained, and discussed regarding a family. My favorite was the time, during my first social service job, when management informed us that the auditors wanted all notes to be typed. Sounds fair enough. Only thing is, ever since I was working there, we were not required to type anything. So guess What I did during that week. You guessed it, I transcribed everything I ever wrote onto a computer. What a fabulous use of my time that week. It was certainly my pleasure to inform all my families that week that I was unavailable to them. I surely had more important things to do with my time.

17

Rubbing people the wrong way

So I briefly mentioned earlier about my arguments
with management over the families rent money. Well, let's
just say that this was something I would further explore
with them, and pretty much every manager, corporate,
supervisor and director from every agency I have worked
for in the past 10 years. I guess, if I was one of the youth I
work with, you would say that I had, trouble with authority
figures.

Maybe it's just my personality. Maybe it's the fact
that, all these years later, I still feel like an outsider in this
field. I always felt that I didn't really belong. I grew up
with a certain structure. A certain mentality. A certain way
to go about your business, work your job, stay organized,
and believe in what you are doing. And, more importantly,
believe that your 'voice' is being heard. And I guess there
remains that part of me that feels as though I deserve more.
I've put everything I have into this field, in this work, and
into these children. For some very selfish reasons, I still
have felt as though I am meant to have more financially. I
believe it's my life long struggle, not just to separate work
from home, but to separate financial reward from emotional
reward.

Plus, I have never fully understood why the people at
the top are always people who never worked in the field.
Does that make any sense? Every agency I ever worked at,
seemed to be run at the top by someone with no social
services experience. Think about it. Would Facebook be
what it is today if Mark Zuckerberg were a culinary major in
college? How much faith would you have in a CEO who
had no idea what it was you were doing, making, creating,
and developing to make him rich? How much could you
rely on such a person to lead your agency, and how much of

a voice do you feel you would have with them?

Anyway, there I go again with the word "voice'. It always applies to the children and families. It also strongly applies to the employee. I remember, a few years ago, once talking with a dedicated co-worker, who was so stressed out over management that she considered quitting. About halfway through her venting, I looked at her and said, "well, how many families would you be helping if you quit?". She immediately stopped what she was saying. In that instant, she realized that she wasn't in it to help the boss get rich. She wasn't in it to get a raise or promotion. She was simply in it to help others succeed. Give others a chance she felt that we all deserved. To this day, she continues her daily efforts to put everything she has into her work, helping families, and changing lives. I often wish I had her heart, her dedication, and her ability to put aside the thoughts of her own success, and simply focus on the success of those we are trying to help. I seem to be too busy worrying about my own success, and my own future.

One of the biggest things I learned about working in social services is that I need to be in it for something other than appreciation. To work in this field, you can't be in it for the money, because you won't make much from it, you can't be in it for the recognition, because you most likely won't really get it, you have to be in it because you want to help others. You have to want equality, respect and appreciation for all, not just yourself. Everyone deserves a chance in life. If society as a whole won't provide that chance, then it's up to certain individuals in that society to help provide that chance.

I'm the one with the New York/Irish/Italian persona. I don't just vent to co-workers, I tell off management. Hey, I never said I was an angel. I just never seemed to agree with what management, state, and counties were doing in regards to the non-profit and the social service industry. Obviously, I never agreed with wasting my time re-writing something I already did because it was easier for auditors to read. I never agreed with waiting for one particular management staff member to sign off on a check that can keep a mother and her son from being homeless, because the other 5 management/middle management staff apparently weren't allowed to sign it. And I certainly never agreed with doing more than what my job description entails, without any financial compensation, simply because it's just considered doing 'whatever it takes', and is supposedly in the best interest of the family at heart. I always hate when they used that against me....although, I kind of used that against the dedicated co-worker I just mentioned to keep her fighting the good fight.

I have always seemed to be at war with someone, even very early on in this field. Always a battle to be fought, outside of courtrooms, outside of schools, and not always a war having to do with the children and families I was hired, and entrusted, to serve. It is this inner battle that has waged on for a decade, causing me loss of sleep, loss of appetite, and loss of desire to fulfill so many other dreams I once had. There have been times when I swear I forgot what I was actually fighting over. Maybe I was just fighting myself. Maybe the real idiot is me. Have I used my work with children to disguise my selfish desires to bring others down who had more than me? Have I used my hard work and excellent documentation as a way to tell off management, get my point across, and not be fired over it? And what does any of that have to do with the work I was hired to do? Maybe I'm the one who doesn't understand how things work, after all. I'm starting to feel like my struggle was internal, and never really involved any of my superiors.

Call of Duty

Well, If mom and her rent was my initiation into nonprofit, and my lack of training was my call of duty, then my 'rite of passage' in this field of work came about a year and a half into my employment. That's when I learned what it was like to be laid off. It was an interesting time in my life. I had already sold my home, due to my pay cut for taking the job after law enforcement, and the bills were piling up on me and my now ex-wife at the time. I was happy to have gone from working 4-midnight, plus working weekends and holidays in the jail, to working 9-5, Monday-Friday, with all holidays off. To me, I saw this as being normal. Working a normal job, for normal hours, and spending the holidays with loved ones. But there I was, sitting in my boss's office, and she begins to tell me, "Ok, well, based on your seniority here (yeah, that's right, working there only a year and half, and I had the most seniority. Explains a lot about nonprofit as well, doesn't it), you will be the last to be laid off. You got a month? "

That period of time has quickly become a distant blur in my life. The one thing I do remember clearly, was going into work every day, reading through the resources I used to help families. Only this time, instead of referring children and families for these agencies services, I was finding their fax numbers and human resources departments in order to apply for jobs with them. What a wonderful use of my time. I'm sure the families I was helping at the time would be pleased to know that I was busy worrying about myself, and leaving them to deal with their struggles and concerns without me.

I don't recall any goodbyes with those families. There were no successes, no graduations, and so all I felt I was really doing was further modeling the idea of abandonment.

The idea that nothing, and no one, is around very long. Just as I learned to build trust, rapport and strength with each family and child, I had to break all of the above to fend for myself. And so what of all my hard work? What of my efforts, my sweat, and my tears, all poured in to each and every child, each and every parent? What did it all amount to? Where was I to go? Did I really want to continue in this field with everything I have learned up to this point. Maybe it was enough. Maybe my 'paid learning' has accumulated the right amount of knowledge I needed, and it was time to learn something new. Or maybe I haven't really finished what I started in my work with children. Maybe I haven't helped enough children yet. Maybe I haven't yet truly helped myself.

On to the next one…and the next one

.

    So off I go into non-profit social services job number 2. Only this time, there's a new word in front of my case manager title. I am now a dependency case manager. Well, talk about not putting your work life into your home life. Let me tell you something, You try keeping that motto with this form of employment. If you don't know what it is, let me tell you. A dependency case manager, to make a long story short, is someone who, technically, has the power to take a child away from their family, place that child in a foster home/group home, and attends court hearings in which they ultimately have the power to permanently take away the parental rights of mom and dad. Yes, ladies and gentlemen, you ultimately can go into court, state your case about what makes mom and dad a bad mom and dad, and can legally have them no longer be mom and dad. How's that for a day job?

    I only worked there for a few months. Same scenario as the first. Hi, I'm Ernest….Hi, I'm Jessica…….here's a list of the 14 families you will be working with. Read their charts/background, call the families…..Good luck…..here I am turning the ignition again and trying not to crash…..Only to soon be told that……yeah…….you guessed it…….the department is being laid off……

    You would think at this point that I would be spending the next 3 months of eventual unemployment finding a new profession. But of course, I did not. Was I just looking to jump into the easiest thing I could, based on my resume, or was it something else? On to the next one. After spending my time being as broke (if not, more broke), then most of the children and families I have been working for, I found myself back on the saddle (or car, so to speak). I began as a case manger again. But later, my department moved into something else. And so began my career in the wonderful world of 'wraparound'.

For those of you who don't know about wraparound, I'll explain it the same way I have been explaining if for years. Remember the old adage, it takes a village to raise a child? Well that's wraparound. It's a process in which you utilize as many people in the community to help you best meet your Childs needs. Yeah, I know, sounds like a great hallmark card, doesn't it?

Now this is when I learned a little bit more about teamwork. Things started off the same. Hi, I'm.......Hi, I'm.........keys....ignition......only this time, I'm not the only one who is always driving.

I have to say, there are many 'benefits' to utilizing the wraparound process to help families. It does make sense. The more, the merrier. If Child A is having a lot of problems, and mother B struggles to resolve those issues, it doesn't necessarily mean that nonprofit staff C will single handedly change the course of this family's life.
Life, in general, is about working together. Life is about sharing in each other's struggles, hardships and triumphs. Life is about being there for someone. Life is about listening. Life is about having your 'voice heard'. (told you, it's a big theme here).

So I'm back 'in the field' again, driving around the city, home to home, family to family, trying to make a difference. But this time, I'm not alone. I have the help of other staff, both employed at my job, and employed elsewhere, to help in this fight. And that is what it's all about, isn't it? Making a difference. It's certainly not about the money. Read your local newspaper. Social services is consistently considered one of the lowest, if not the lowest, paid profession in America. Although, if you do your research correctly, you will notice that everyone on the corporate level of 'non-profit' all make over $100,000/year. But I guess, for the purposes of this book, and my sanity, that is beside the point.

The point is this: What price do you put on someone's life? What price do you put on their chances to succeed? What's it worth to have even one child find success with help from others? I remember hearing an analogy from a friend years ago regarding his own life, and the concept of time. He put it like this,

"Think of it this way, I can drive from Los Angeles to Las Vegas in about 4 hours. Or, I can book a flight, and be there in less than 1. Sure, It's more expensive to fly, but I am saving about 3 hours of my life that I can't get back. So I said to myself, what is my life worth to me? Well, certainly worth having 3 more extra hours of not sitting in a car." I feel as though this applies to the world of social services. Only this time, it's not your own life, it's about the lives of others. It's about helping a young child avoid spending the next 6 months of their lives in a detention center. Isn't their life worth saving? We in this field all try to save every life we can. But maybe that was the problem in the first place. Why do most in the field consider it so black and white? Why must it only be success or failure? Can such pressure get to an employee in this field? For me, the answer is yes. For me, that pressure has caused much heartache, distress and chaos. Not just chaos at work, but chaos at home.

Now, there are a lot of stereotypes out there about the kind of people who work in this field. And yes, I'm willing to admit, some of them seem to be true. Many of us are nuts. I've seen coworkers lash out at each other, lash out at management...yeah, besides me...and even lash out at families. This is the one I never understood. Why would you yell at a family. To me, it doesn't matter what good or harm they are doing at the time. We are but employees of a company. We are there to build up, not break down. And, no matter what the title on your business card says, we have no true authority over any child, parent or family. There are those out there who I feel continue to abuse this authority, day in, day out, and seem to only put more pressure on the family then they already have. However, despite the misgivings of some in this field, for most, the purpose remains the same. Whether that employee is in it for the family, the child, or their own sense of self-worth, the bottom line is that they are there. They are working, they are dedicated, and they are involved in what they do, how they do it, and understand that compensation is more emotional then financial.

It's hard enough, apparently in this country, to truly care for and protect our children. So imagine what it is to be out there, traveling the city, being a protector of someone else's child.

Why we do what we do

So why do it? Well, I guess that brings me back to the story I alluded to earlier of the young man in court. There I was, a few weeks before that hearing, listening to the emotional story of a crying mother, explaining the current circumstances that are her life. And during this turmoil, and during this process of getting it from all angles: school, social services, and the Department of Children and family services, there was also a legal case against her then teenage son. A young man who, at the time, was facing up to 3 years in a detention youth camp, for fighting another student. Oh, I bet you didn't think your kid could be arrested for that, huh? Well, you can if the kid you hit doesn't so easily get back up off the ground.

So, what to do? Do I judge the kid for what he has done? Do I blame the absent father? Do I blame the mother for not trying hard enough when I don't even know her or her family?. Or do I not only do my job, but also do what is in the best interest of a youth in our society, without judgment or bias? And, most importantly, never forget to empower the family to be part of the solution.

I decided to put in my 'time'. I went into court, learned more about the situation, and basically swore to a judge, under oath, that I would help find the right resources to help this young man. Day after day, week after week, I learned about this family. I learned their strengths, I learned their weaknesses. And we worked together to build solutions. I got to know this family on such a personal level. You have to realize how it feels to work a job where you hear every little detail about a family's life. Stories that you think are only fiction, made for TV. But these are the deepest, darkest, most heartfelt stories that you can imagine. And, all the while, I notice something during these conversations. As time went on, and as this kid began to grow, I realized something. I realized that, despite it all, there is still laughter. There are the days when this young man would blast the music in my car on the way back to his home from school. There were the jokes, the family sit-downs, games, and belief of hope. Hope in the better tomorrow. Hope in the fact that life really isn't all that bad. And sitting around all day thinking about the consequences for past actions will get you nowhere.

And so I learned from that strength and resilience. I used that openness and desire to succeed. I used that sense of humor to fuel me, as much as them, to fight their battle. And, about two years later, years spent fighting the courts, changing the young man's school, and finding every resource imaginable for teens and single moms, I sat in that courtroom, waiting to hear what were the result of everyone's hard work. I don't remember the judges' words, exactly, but what I do remember is this. I remember the words, "case dismissed". So begins the new life of a young man. A young man who now has 3 extra years of his time to use. A successful end to a possible bad situation. I found out later that the young man, who when I met him was a straight 'F' student in the 9th grade, would go on to graduate from high school. His mother would eventually move out of a home she was sharing with other relatives, and have her own home. A home in which her children could have their own space, their own privacy, and their own inner peace. He probably makes more money than I do right now, but who's complaining.

28

What is success?

Success, however, can be the exception to the rule, not the norm, in the world of social services. Although, how do you really define success anyway? Does a child have to stay out of juvenile hall, graduate high school, or be returned from a foster home to his biological family for your time with them to be a success?

Life, as we know, is not as simple as a quick beginning, middle and end. Life, like the idea of wraparound, is a process. And that process can last ones entire lifetime. If I could give one quick word of advice to all current social services employees, it would be this: Don't ever judge your success on graduations, case dismissed judgments, or family reunification. Base your own success on your own ability to remain consistent, remain humble, and remain a support to those you work for.

Think of it in terms of your own childhood. I can't tell you how many times I did something that is deemed to be wrong. And yet, I did it anyway. But I always tried to learn from my mistakes. I learned how to do better, how to be better, and most importantly, I learned to understand what it was to have a role model. Someone to listen to, someone to be believe in. That is where the success comes in. Success is not always seen 'in the moment'. Success can be role modeled, learned, and eventually understood. Think about it. We are now in the new age of Facebook. So I ask you this: How many of you have reconnected with old middle school and high school friends from years past? How many of those young men and women were once known for their aggressiveness, struggle, and defiant behaviors? Now, how many of them are 'grown-ups', living in the suburbs, with a spouse, with children, with a life that some may even feel is a success?

They may not all have found their American Dream, but maybe I haven't either. So what? Again, what do you define as success

What are we all to be remembered for?

What do you want to be remembered for? About 6 months after I had already quit my job as a correctional officer, I was walking around a local Walmart shopping for groceries. All of a sudden, an extremely large man came walking over to me. He said, "Hey Mr. dove?" Now, seeing as how I was still in my 20s, and this man had to be at least in his 30s, the whole Mr. Dove thing threw me off. And, apparently, I must have stood there frozen like I was currently in a childhood game of freeze tag, because he called me out on it immediately. He said, "you don't remember me, huh, yeah, I didn't think you would. I was locked up in jail for a bit. Anyway, I never had a problem with you. You were always respectful to everyone in there. I guess that's all I wanted to say, sorry to bother you. Have a nice day".

To this day, I will always remember that encounter. Not because of the instant scared-out-of-my-mind-moment I had before he said everything was cool, but because I learned something that day. I learned something that 3 years working in that jail, and 10 years working in social services could not have ever taught me any better. I learned about respect. I learned about how to treat a person, and I learned how to be a role model. I learned that, as we teach these troubled youth today, we truly are responsible for our actions. And whether we are modeling to an 8 year child, or for a 68 year old grandmother, we will forever be modeling to others. And it's not always what we teach them that is important, it's how they remember us that may be the key to their success.

What have I learned?

 So what have I learned in 10 years working in this field? My college degree is in Criminal Justice. I never went back to school to learn about children and families. I never tried to obtain a license to become a licensed clinical social worker. What I did was learn from my experiences. For me, I never felt the need to pay for further education. Not when I can learn everything I need to out in the field. No book can teach you how to remain calm, cool, and focused in the middle of family chaos. No book can teach you how to sit in a courtroom, and explain just how well a young man has done to change his life around, because you were there every step of the way. Anybody can read a book, retain the information, and pass a few tests. Not everyone can handle 40 hours a week of helping a mother pay her rent, helping a child stay out of jail, and helping a grandfather understand that he alone can still make all the difference in the world to a teenage girl he feels he just can't relate to. Maybe what I've learned most is about strength, courage, and determination. I'm not just talking about the families I worked with, I'm talking about myself. I've learned about how to handle struggle, how to handle a crisis, and most importantly, and most unfortunately, I've learned about how to deal with failure.

 They say one major thing you can never truly learn, until you have one of your own, is how to be a parent. I, for one, still do not yet have a child. If and when I am ever blessed with a child, will I know what to do? What is the right thing to do, anyway? I've seen it all. I've seen single mom's struggle. I've seen single mom's succeed. I've seen two-parent households struggle. I've seen two-parent households succeed. I've seen a family making minimum wage struggle with a defiant child, and I've seen a family making over $150,000/year struggle with the same thing. So what is the answer? There may not truly be a right answer. But, to me, there are things that 'couldn't hurt to try'.

Voice:

In the end, don't we just all want to be heard?
Whether they are a 6 year old girl, or a 17 year old young
man, you can just see it in their eyes. My first attempt at
giving advice to parents is to not only listen to your child,
but learn to understand your child. Whether you respond
by saying everything right, or everything wrong, just don't
forget to respond.

As an employee in social services, it is our job to
listen, understand, and respond. The benefit of being on
that side of the field, so to speak, is that we can have the
added knowledge, experience and resources to help in the
situation and bring about successful outcomes. On the other
side, with success also comes failure. And, as long as you
work in nonprofit, one thing you will have to come
accustomed to is failure. Although, what truly constitutes
failure?

A few years ago, I worked with a teenage boy
involved in the court system. When it came to the last few
months of his court case, all the judge really wanted was for
this young man to attend school regularly, and he would be
taken off of probation. While working with this young man,
all he ever really said was that he didn't like school. So,
what did we all do as a staff, as a team, as a unit. We got
together, lived the motto of 'whatever it takes'. This
involved myself, along with another coworker, personally
traveling to this young man's home, about 7:45am each
mooring, Monday-Friday, and transporting him to school,
whether he liked it or not. So what happened during these
three months? He attended school of course. During those
three months, the 5 days a week transport became 3 days a
week. Then one day a week. Then it was up to mom to get
him ready, and only call if he refused to go. But he went,

every day, for the remainder of the time before court. At the court hearing, I sat in the room, and heard those favorite two words that all employees, and of course families, want to hear, "case dismissed". Sounds like success, doesn't it? Well, about 3 months later, after we graduated the family from services, we come to find out that the same young man had dropped out of school, and refused to attend the alternative school, where he would only have to attend a school program 2 days a week. Last I heard, he was 19 years old, still a high school dropout, and is currently hanging out at a friend's house doing drugs. So, what happened? On paper, this young man was a 'success'. however, like I've been saying, what is considered success? If I was listening to this young man, I would have heard someone speak of not wanting school, not wanting the structure, the early hours and the social aspect of being around so many others Children. Maybe I could have helped the family explore other options. Maybe I could have helped this young man obtain employment, maybe...

In my opinion, I don't think you have truly understood the field of social service and nonprofit until you spend an hour, in a family's home, watching as mom cries, child lashes out, and you try to stay in the middle. All the while trying your best to calm the situation, help the situation, and resolve the situation. And then, just as you are leaving the home with mom crying, child lashing out, and the families rent and electric bill still not having yet been paid, you immediately drive to the next house, 15 minutes away. You then spend the next hour in that home...And then, you immediately drive to the next house, 30 minutes away, and you spend the next hour in that home...It is at this point that you are truly working in nonprofit. There's no time for self. There's no time for reflection. There's no time for looking back. There is only time to gather up your thoughts, change your mindset, and begin to focus on the next one. As is real life, this kind of day, for me, was about learning to place focus on others, no matter how different the scenario, and rely on my own strength to stay in the present, minute by minute, hour by hour, moment by moment. Because if you lose focus for even a second, you might miss that one chance at success.

If not for money, why still do it?

I love to use the word non-profit, because it may be one of the worst examples of an oxymoron. The term nonprofit, simply means that, at the end of the day, the money that went into the business/agency has to go directly back out. But what you forget to realize is this. There is no better way to take the money back out then by putting it into someone's salary. However, it's not the social service worker who gets it. It is the social service Director who gets that big piece of the pie.

But again, this book is not about those who are receiving what they have not truly earned, even though I seem to be making a big effort to point that out. This book...this story, is about those of us who are receiving something other than money. Those of us seeking change. Not some political motto to get elected. This change honestly is for the benefit of someone else. This change is meant to help children find their own version of happiness and success. This change I have spent years trying to develop in others. This change is something I struggled so hard for to develop in myself.

Whenever someone asks me why I do what I do, I usually tell them the same thing. I always give them a scenario. I can't help it, answering them is too easy, or maybe too complicated: "Have you ever seen a homeless man/woman on the street, talking to themselves, and sleeping on the sidewalk?" "Well, did you ever stop to think that maybe that 40 year old homeless man/woman was once a child. A child with a mental health issue. A mental health issue which was never treated. Which led to time in juvenile hall, which led to dropping out of school, which led to..."

Life is not just a process, it's a journey. And, believe it or not, we have more control over the success of others on that journey then we realize. We have the power to help build the roads necessary to further along someone's journey, steer them in the right direction, and watch as they truly find their way. They may not all succeed, but with guidance, support, and role modeling, at least they will have their chance. You can't always help someone find themselves when they are lost, but you can help them realize that they are worth saving.

Children aren't the only ones lost and looking to be found

Throughout this journey, I myself have felt just as lost, hopeless and weak as anyone. We are, again, only but employees of a job in the end. We become so involved and personally invested when dealing with children and families that we often forget about that part of it. There were days when I would be in my car, outside of a child's home or school, crying. Not because of anything negative with the child or family. It was simply the case of a man being overwhelmed with emotion. A man questioning his employment, his purpose, and his reasons for being there in the first place. I would think to myself, what is the point? I'm broke. I don't own a home, I can't do anything special even if I took a vacation, and I can't take the pressure of someone else's failure anymore. It was during times like these when I learned about my own strength, my resilience, and my ability to truly put others first through listening. Listening, and caring, about what others have to say. Also remembering that I too deserve success. I too deserve to be heard. I too can handle what is being thrown at me in life, because I have seen others handle far worse. These families have become my role models. I have learned more from them then they have ever learned from me. These are tools that I've used, not only to help children and families, but to be a better friend, a better son, and a better husband. These are skills I would have never truly learned if not for being in this field of work. These are skills I hope to keep for the rest of my life.

I am now, for the second time, a married man. My wife always seems to make it a point to tell everyone about one of the main reasons why our marriage works. She always says, "my husband is a great communicator". It is this skill of communication, this skill of listening, and this skill of really hearing what others have to say, that has allowed me the opportunity to share the rest of my life with the woman of my dreams. I now have her as my role model. I share my dreams with her. I share my hopes with her. She is my success. I've succeeded because she and I are together. I've succeeded because I found happiness, not just in her, but in myself when I am around her. I've said in this story that's it's hard to define success. Well, for me, success is found in my love for her. Success is found in my love for myself, and it will be defined by our ever growing relationship with each other, and by how we model our success to others.

Honesty truly is the best policy

Let's go back to the whole idea of listening, and the concept of one's voice being heard. A few years ago, I was working with an African American teenager. I, myself, am Caucasian. The family was involved in the dependency court system, which meant that the state was 'keeping an eye on the family", with possible consequences of taking this young man away from his family if mom didn't show that she was capable of meeting his needs. So, in I go, to the home, starting a new family on a new journey. So what did this journey entail. Well, for the first few months, it entailed me being ridiculed, made fun of, verbally abused, and having racial terms be thrown at me on a weekly basis by this young man. What did I do in return? I came to the home every week, greeted him back with, "good afternoon", and said things like, "I'm just trying to help", or "why are you doing this to me?". It's times like this that I remember once again why every experience is a learning experience. Remember, I spent 3 years of my life working in a jail. So I've seen it all, heard it all, and dealt with it all. I learned how to take in information, and take in certain negative words as nothing but 'noise'. So I learned to ignore it. I learned to adapt to it. I learned to be immune from it.

Honestly, it wasn't until about 4 or 6 months later that the young man taught me something invaluable to me in my life today. He said, "if I'm really bothering you, why don't you just come out and say it? I had no idea at the time what he meant. He could obviously see I was bothered by it every time. I always responded with the Why, really, not again, etc. But what I didn't realize was, I should have immediately said, "please stop, I am offended by what you are saying, and I am not comfortable being here with you listening to these remarks" So that's what I finally managed

41

to do, and say, to this young man. He was never inappropriate with me again.

I just learned an invaluable lessen from a 16 year old child. Sometimes, in life, it can seem as though we are being manipulated, mistreated, harassed, and abused. And, in many cases, that can be true. But, at the same time, what you can be hearing is a young man who, out of obvious mistrust of a stranger anyway, will say what he wants, when he wants. He may not truly understand that you are intimidated, scared, or offended, unless you flat out tell him that. Because, again, you are the stranger. You are the person, who, in their eyes, is getting paid a bunch of money…yeah, for some reason, most families think we get paid well to do this…to talk to them, and so you are not really worried about what mean things they have to say, because they don't really matter.

So, I learned. I learned to speak up for myself. I learned, not to just ignore others, but to respond to others. It is that response to others which can, in many ways, show your respect towards them. And, not only did I learn these things, but I was paid to learn. The great Dallas Mavericks owner Mark Cuban would be proud.

Discipline

Everyone always wonders the same thing as parents: How do I discipline my child? In this day and age of hotlines, 800 numbers, and the department of Child and Family Services, it seems as though every child, at any age, has that number on speed dial, on their own cell phones (best part is defiant kids still earning cell phones somehow). So what do you do? Well, you know what, the concept of 'timeout' really isn't as corny and old fashioned as it sounds, at least when it comes to the little ones.

Here is the thing about timeout. Here is something I learned working in this field all these years. Timeout does not mean putting a 6 year old child in the corner for 30 minutes. That's just plain unrealistic. A 6 year old just can't be placed into a spot for 30 minutes straight, and then all of sudden understand about the punishment, and never do the defiant behave again.

You have to start off with more realistic goals, consequences and expectations. You may have to even start at 30 seconds, not 30 minutes.

Think about it in terms of teaching someone a new language. If you were Spanish speaking, and you wanted to teach someone who isn't. Would you sit them in a room, say an entire paragraph of words to them, and ask them to repeat it back? Or would you say one word, and have them repeat that one word back to you?

You can't truly begin to teach someone something, unless they fully understand what it is they are supposed to be learning. I learned a lot about this over my years working in this field. You can't role model something to a child that you yourself don't truly understand. You can't simply 'wing it', make it up as you go along, and expect positive outcomes. If you don't fully invest in what it is you are teaching someone, then they may not truly learn from it. Not only that, they may see in your face that you don't really believe in it either.

Knowledge is power

When I first moved to California back in 2007, I
quickly took the first job I could. It was working with adults
who have schizophrenia. I only worked there for a few
months. Let's just say I had a few choice words for a lazy
boss, and the higher ups weren't too happy about that.
Anyway, I remember learning one invaluable lesson. I
learned about body language. I learned that, no matter what
you are telling certain people, there are those who can read
you like a book. There are those who can see right through
the lies, right through the crap you might be making up, and
right through attempts to care about what you are saying. If
I was sick, they knew it. If I had received a phone call from
back home that made me sad, they felt it. If I didn't believe
in the topic of discussion I was teaching them that day, they
sensed it. I had to learn quickly about the idea of true
professionalism. I learned about the importance of taking
your job seriously, leaving your troubles elsewhere, and
focusing everything on the task at hand.

It is not just those with a mental illness who seem to
have this gift. I've seen it in children throughout my time
working in this field. Children of all ages, and children from
two opposite sides of the country.

You'd be amazed at how attentive and even insightful
our youth of today are. Not just any youth, but youth who
have been ignored. Youth who have been abused. And
youth who have been alone. These are the youth that make
up our society today. It is our duty to respect these youth,
respect their insightfulness, and respect the fact that they are
willing and able to call you out on your half-hearted
attempts to help. These children never ask for my help.
They never want to trust me, and they never want to believe
in me. All I can do is earn that trust, and earn that belief by

truly believing in what it is I am trying to do for them. Their words must be important to me. I must be a good listener. I must be a good communicator, especially in my marriage, apparently. I take this knowledge with me everywhere I go. I use this knowledge every chance I get. If I feel that placing a child in time out is a good idea, I am able to fully express that to a child and their family. They will believe that I believe. They will accept it. They will learn from it. If it doesn't work, and the family feels they have a better idea, I will respect that idea. I will believe in their idea, and I will support their idea.

It's not just about teaching that child a lesson, it's about helping that child understand that there will always be a consequence for a bad behavior. And whether you are doing it through 30 minutes, 5 minutes, yelling, or screaming, the only response you are supposed to be modeling is "please don't do that again". By screaming, yelling, and even abuse, what you often are teaching the child is, "hey, apparently, the world stops when I do A, but when I do B, nothing really happens, good or bad. So maybe I should keep doing A, because that's when mommy and daddy pay me the most attention. When it leads to abuse, that abuse begins to define them. That abuse controls them. That abuse ruins everything that could have been built up in that child, and everything that could have led to that Childs success.

I remember one time, while visiting a child at his middle school, he began to jump up and down in his chair. He began to count as he did it. All the while, looking right at me. So, what did I do? I couldn't put him in time out. I couldn't take away any items or privileges, so, I watched. I watched him, up and down, up and down, until he got to 100. And then? He went back to answering my questions about how he was doing, how school was, how his mom was doing, etc. They say patience is a virtue. Well, when dealing with children, patience is a must.

Along with patience, comes respect. Not just respect for what a child or family has, but respect for what they don't have. Another thing I learned in life is that you can't truly punish a child with a consequence of taking things away, if that child doesn't really have anything to take.

One of the hardest parts about my work with children is seeing what it is that they go through in their day to day lives just to survive. Growing up, my family was never rich, but we were also never poor. I never received every single game I wanted, but I did receive games. As a teenager, I was never given a brand new car, but they assisted in buying me a used one. I always knew the value of a dollar, but I also had the advantage of having access to that dollar, and the ability to learn what to do with it when I had it.

Here I am, years later, working with a family to find a negative consequence for a child who has nothing. No toys, no working TV, and no driver's license, let alone a car. This is why I feel that, punishment or no punishment, time out or no time out, one of the biggest things to do is acknowledge your child either way. Acknowledge the fact that you feel what they did was wrong. And later acknowledge to them the fact that you still love them. Because, in the end, one of the best things in life is love. You can give that to your children for free.

Support

If I've learned anything working with children, it is
that you can't really accomplish much on your own. We all
need a little help sometimes. Life, as we know it, has always
been built on the strengths, supports, and determination of a
team of others. People may always be grouped into terms
such as leaders and followers. But without followers to
build a solid foundation, there would be no place to lead.
Picture working with a team of people: A team of minds,
working on the same project, proposal, and idea. Picture in
your mind the possible arguments, struggles, and differences
of opinion that goes on in such a team environment, even if
for the better good of the project at hand. Now imagine that
'project' is a 6 year old child. A hyperactive, overly friendly,
abused 6 year old child. What then? What you have now is
more than a project. More than an idea, and more than a
projection of gains and profit. How hard would you work to
help that child gain success? Would you listen to the ideas
and opinions of others, if it was for the benefit of a child?
I've learned, not only from children and families, but from
co-workers as well. If home life involves seeking assistance,
guidance and support from family and friends, then work
life should involve doing the same. We all have a lot to give
as far as experience, knowledge and expertise. We all have
our weaknesses, but we also all have our strengths. I've
learned over the years how important it is to find those
strengths in my co-workers, and have the ability to ask them
for help, and use that help to support a child.
There's no legal probation court system when it
comes to 6 year olds. No measure of success to be shown by
a graduation from high school, or obtaining of employment.
This is where the real work begins. The work of having a
hand in further developing the progress of a child. This may

be, and has always been, the hardest cases for me to be on.

It is during this time that there must always be an all-for-one-one-for-all mentality to support that child. No matter your age, education, or license, the bottom line is that you are not what's important, the child is. I feel that this simple concept often gets lost in the field of social services. We are, in the end, a group of individuals. We are men, women, fathers, mothers, and most of all, employees. It's the one thing that so many forget to realize. Employee. What you are doing is a job. This child is not your child. It takes a village to raise a child. But this child is not of 'your' village. You are, above all things, providing a service to the family. But, inevitably, what many in the field provide is usually their heart, their emotions, and their all. And that effort, when combined with the idea of working in a group with others, can often lead to disagreements, miscommunication, and sometimes anger. This anger causes us to lose focus on what is most important. This child. What makes a great team, and support system, is a positive combination of the sum of its parts. If at least one of those parts is always faltering, then what you are truly trying to build, which is success in a child, will never work.

Leaving your emotions at home.

It is one of the toughest things to do when working
with children. Our emotions are what drive us. Our
emotions are often what motivate us to succeed. But, in the
case of the child, it is not ourselves that we are helping.
Early on in my career, I found it much easier to separate
these emotions. Once that theoretical 9am hit, I was all
about family. Calls were made, resources were found, visits
were conducted. However, when that final tick tock struck
at 5pm, I was all about me.

Meanwhile, all around me, I saw emotions. I saw
stress, I saw anger, and I saw desperation from co-workers
on a daily basis. Through those first few years, I saw many
dedicated employees come and go. I saw some quit due to
the work. I saw some quit due to their anger towards
supervisors. I saw some quit due to the fact that they could
not fully separate their emotions.

I even found myself helping others in this regard. I
acted as a role model to them, modeling how I go about my
job. Modeling how I document my work, account for my
work, and put my work completely behind me at the end of
the day. I even remember, on one occasion, my supervisor
questioned my efforts based on my lack of emotions. I was
speaking to my supervisor about a child. One who was in
turmoil. This girl was in danger of being kicked out of
school. Her father was broke, and she was damaging their
home on a daily basis. I updated my supervisor on these
events, discussed strategies being worked on, and discussed
strategies to use for the coming week. It was during this
conversation that she looked me right in the eye and said,
"You don't seem too emotional about this. It's as if you
almost don't really care about this poor child". I obviously
took offense to the comment. (especially since I caught that

same supervisor numerous times playing solitaire on her computer, taking 2 hour lunches with another supervisor, and arguing with her own daughter on the phone half the time). However, I didn't argue. I simply stated that I'm doing the best I can to help, and being more emotionally involved with the situation probably wouldn't help the child, so I choose to focus on strategies and resolutions to the problem. Wow, looking back on it now, I almost wish I was still that guy. That guy who cared, but didn't become overwhelmed by it. That guy who wished every family success, but didn't lose sleep over their failure. That guy who, despite what may have been going on around him in his personal life, always was able to focus on his families for eight hours every day. I kind of miss that guy.

Think about it. How often do you have a bad night, or a bad weekend? How often do you yourself become financially unable to pay a bill, or hurt your arm, or break up with your boyfriend/girlfriend? And when that happens, how do you feel that next day at work? Do you work slower? Do you work angry? Do you have in your mind the idea that if you can just get through these last couple of days as quickly as possible, you can enjoy your weekend and give yourself some well-deserved 'self-care'? Well, now picture having one of those things happening to you, and then spending the next eight hours of your day listening to a mother telling you their child overdosed on drugs, was arrested at school, or was taken from their home in the middle of the night due to allegations of abuse. Are you still thinking about just making it through the day now?

I have since spent the latter part of my ten years of service in this field fighting to keep things separated. To not take things too personally, and to not be so fully invested in these families. No longer am I the young man in that supervisor's office, stating the issues at hand, and brain storming the solution to resolve those issues. I am now the man who often takes those matters to heart, takes those matters personally, and makes it my responsibility to resolve those matters at any cost to save a life. It is true that we can be led by our emotions. We can be fueled by those emotions. We can also be drained by those emotions. How can I not. This is not just some model plane I am constructing. One in which I can simply come back the next day and finish. If a child becomes broken, you cannot simply go to the store and buy another one. You cannot simply come into work a little early the next day and make it look better. I always seemed to find myself making everything my responsibility. It's my task to complete. My child to save. My family to help. Only, it wasn't my child. It wasn't my family. In the end, success or failure, the child would be gone from my life eventually. Where do all those emotions go then?

Saying Goodbye

I once worked with a child and his family for over 3 years. I watched him grow, literally. I watched him mature, and learn. Learn from his mistakes. Begin to truly understand what is going on around him. And begin to succeed in building a stronger education for himself and for his future. I used to drive 60 miles roundtrip, weekly, listening to the family argue, complain, and threaten that it may be best if the child were somewhere else, only to change their mind the next week and want him to stay. 3 summers driving in 90+ degree heat, in a car with no air conditioning. 3 years of not only keeping them together, but 3 years of keeping myself together by not blowing up out of frustration when they didn't seem to listen to each other. But then, in what seemed like an instant, it was over.

You plan ahead. You talk about the day. And the day comes. You have a party. You celebrate the child's achievements, you award him some kind of make-shift reward/certificate, and then you say goodbye. And then what? What of all the hard work. What of all the loyalty and dedication that a team of staff provided to this family. All the advice given, all the advice taken. Suddenly, it's all over. What do you do next?

Well, you start all over again with a new child. One with so much to learn. Parents with so much anger that matches their child's anger. I begin to drive more miles to their home. Another summer spent in a hot car, another hour spent in a family home trying to keep one parent from yelling at the other, and one child from yelling at another. I feel like I am right back where I started. I feel like I haven't accomplished anything. That is when the emotions completely take over my life. That is when I feel lost. That is when I feel like I have nothing. That is when my struggle continues.

Self-care

Which brings me to the idea/concept of self-care. How many of us out there practice self-care? And when I mean self-care, I don't mean self-medicate. I'm talking about truly taking care of yourself on a regular basis. This may be the most important concept, practice and idea when it comes to succeeding in having any kind of long term career when working with children and families. I've spent years trying to figure this out.

It's amazing how often in this field, like many other fields I'm sure, we find ourselves teaching others about self-care, but never practicing it ourselves. I can't tell you how many times I've seen dedicated, amazing and loyal employees spend hours, days, and weeks helping a child develop some form of self-care to best meet their needs. They may have enrolled the child into a summer camp, karate class, or soccer team. They may have purchased art supplies, books, and music cd's, and role modeled how to best utilize these items to improve their behaviors, calm their anger, and strengthen their resolve to make it through hard times. And yet, when the day is over, those same dedicated staff find themselves at home, alone, sitting on a couch watching whatever pops on first, and letting their anger over boyfriends, girlfriends, hurt arms and money consume them.

You can never forget to practice what you preach. Besides, we all know that you can't really help others unless you can first help yourself. Well, maybe I really never knew that for a long time. I guess I always thought about it in terms of self-esteem. How can I truly be successful unless I truly believe in myself. All I felt I needed was the right job, the right amount of money, and the right physical appearance to obtain what I wanted. During this time, I never seemed to think about it in terms of helping a child. In terms of putting personal things aside, and being content enough in my life to simply be pleasant towards others.

To simply be satisfied in where I am, what I am doing, and show that in my body language to a child looking for happiness. How can I achieve something that seems so simple, yet so hard to accomplish? I've always had the ability to make others laugh, but how do I accomplish it without first only seeing myself as a clown?

My outlet has always been my writing. It's not only a way to express myself, but a way to test myself. I would often sit in front of my laptop, looking at a blank screen. I would then begin to research and find a quote from some old movie I enjoyed watching. And then, after I've found my favorite quote, I would sit there and write an entire blog, using that quote, and sharing a specific idea and thought related to it.

There were days when I would struggle to find the right words. Heck, there were days I would struggle just to find the right quote. But the purpose was the same. The purpose was to challenge myself. Prove to myself that I have a talent. Prove that my talent is more than just a hobby, it's a way to 'get away'. Be in my own head. Be in my own world. Enjoy every minute of that world. A world in which everything I have to say is important. Not just important to the readers, but important to me. It will forever be my coping skill, my strategy, and my intervention on myself. There has never been a better way to produce more positive results in myself then by challenging myself in the form of writing.

In this world, there are no children to save. No parents to help. No promotion to fight for. In this world, I am free. I am free to imagine. I am free to be, and write, whatever I wish. In writing, for me, there is no work involved. There is no 'eight and hit the gate' mentality.

There is no need to take a mental health day. For me, there is no better way to improve my mental health then by expressing my thoughts onto paper. Success, in my eyes, is not found in the article itself, but in the fact that I was writing it in the first place.

My other form of self-care has always been comedy. During the past couple of years, I have used this form of self-care as my way to vent. Not necessarily about the job, the bosses, or the agency, but to vent out about life in general, and how I perceive it. Sometimes, you just have to have a sense of humor just to make it through the day. There is also a challenge that goes with this form of self-care as well. The challenge of public speaking. The challenge of expressing your thoughts to complete strangers, and hoping that they find the humor in what you are saying. It's yet another challenge I deal with head on. I may put as much work into my self-care as I do the work I accomplish at my job, but I've always expected nothing from others in my writing and in my comedy. There's no complaining about my pay, my bosses and my lack of accomplishing certain goals, unless it makes for a good joke. All I need is a pen and paper. All I need is one Microphone. All I want is the chance to love myself and what I do to challenge myself, all the while using it as my coping skill to remain sane while being surrounded by such chaos.

It doesn't hurt to use that sense of humor while working with children and families either. What better way to 'lighten up things' in a room with a distraught family then to begin and end every conversation with humor.

This is how I have personally chosen to deal with my emotions at times. Again, I challenge myself. Only this time, it's not a blank page in front of me. it's a distraught mother of 3. So now, how do I best take that challenge? How do I find humor in the situation? How do I make a crying mother laugh? For me, this is best form of therapy I can every really give to a family. Just as my families have taught me, I have taught my families that life goes on. There can humor in anything. I've learned that if you can't make fun of others, make fun of yourself . Children always seem to love when I make fun of myself. At the end of the day, when all feels lost, I still have my laptop waiting for me at home. I still have access, throughout the city of Los Angeles, to a microphone. Give me a pen and paper, or give me a stage. Either way, you've given me hope. You've given me happiness. You've given me life.

My change. My struggle.

As the years have passed, I've seen a change in my own behaviors, mood and personality. It seems as though my emotional separation of work life from home life has started to crumble. No longer have I been so easily able to 'keep my work at work'. I think it's just human nature to care. To care for others in need. Especially when you're 'on the front lines' so to speak, and seeing what is truly going on in the world, in your city, and in your community. It's as though I see myself becoming the ones I've always seen over the years who have left the field of social services. I see the overwhelmingness in myself these days. I can feel the why me, why here, why now. That 'why today' mentality coming over me more and more. I'm more regularly becoming that guy again in the car crying, minutes away from starting another counseling session with a struggling child, all the while struggling myself. Struggling to find my own happiness. Struggling to find my own new motivation. Every day I fight to convince children throughout the city to get off that bed and make something of themselves. All the while, I struggle with that 'it's Monday' look on my face.

Life will always have its ups and downs, but what if your job is to work with other peoples ups and downs? You may hold your anger in, but you can't let a child do the same. You may take a 'mental health day' off from work on a Monday or Friday to extend your weekend, but you must also somehow continue to encourage a child to not miss a day of school. You may take a 2 week vacation at a nice resort to recharge your batteries, but you must also try and convince a child to walk to the park for an hour to recharge theirs. You never really know what you have, until you see the possessions of others. You never really see yourself for who you are, and what you can become, until you see it in the eyes of a child. Their strength has always given me hope. Their hope has always made me feel success. Their success, no matter how few and far between, has given me the reason to stay.

And that is what working with children is all about. It's about seeing what they have, seeing what they go through, and helping them create a different environment for themselves. It's about helping them create their own getaway, their own self-care, and develop the kind of skills that will change the course of their lives. It's about doing whatever you can to prevent a young man from missing his opportunity in life. It's about helping him find his own success, and helping him avoid failure.

Accepting failure:

Success, as I've stated throughout this book, is hard to define, but easy to accept. Whether I was sitting in a courtroom watching a child be given another chance, or sitting in a high school auditorium watching a child graduate high school, I can see, with my own eyes, a form of success. I can see that light at the end of the tunnel in a child's eyes. And I can see the thankfulness in their eyes. I can acknowledge that something positive has occurred, and I am happy to be a part of it.

But what about failure. How do you even define failure? And, most importantly, how do you deal with it when working with children? I can't tell you how many times I have gone to a court room, sat and listened to a judge praise a child for their hard work and progress. Some judges even make it a point to not only thank the family, but also the social service worker present, for their hard work and dedication. That is when you feel success. And then, the next day, same courthouse, same courtroom, different child. Only this time, the judge is reviewing a child with poor school attendance, poor grades, poor behaviors at home, and a positive drug test taken. And as I watched such a child be handcuffed, and taken away kicking and screaming to be detained, I think to myself, is that failure?

I mean, who is to blame? Do you blame the child? Do you blame the parent? Do you blame yourself? They say you can't accept success without also accepting failure, but what if that failure involves the life of a child. It's not like baseball, where you can get a hit one out of every 3 at bats, and be considered an all-star. Every life counts. I've seen a lot of commercials promoting that, 'failure is not an option'. Well, sometimes, that option is taken away from you. It's put into someone else's hands. How can I go on accepting that fact? How can I continue to accept the perceived failure in others? How can I not put those perceived failures on myself? How can I continue to put those apparent losses behind me, and continue on?

You can never forget the losses…

Whether fair or not, it is the losses that will forever be my burden to keep. I will carry them with me wherever I go. Every incarceration, every high school dropout, and every child 'left behind' through no fault of their own, i.e. me getting laid off, will remain my burden to carry. I will always be haunted by the memories of lost youth. For every success, I take no credit. For every failure, I take responsibility. So is the burden of a man whose put pressure on himself his whole life. They say pressure only increases motivation. I say pressure only enhances fear. The fear of failure is what really drives us. It's that fear that keeps you going, keeps you working, and keeps you alive. Funny how life seems to be something you cannot really count on, but fear is always there. You may ask yourself, why a man would place such a burden on himself for so long. I may never be able to answer that question. But I can tell you this, I remember the day that child was taken away in an ambulance to be sent to a psychiatric hospital. I remember the day that child overdosed on drugs. Yeah, I remember the day I helped keep a mother and her son in their home that first year, but I also remember the day another family looked to me for more financial assistance, and I could only look on and watch as they move out of their apartment, and into a homeless shelter.

I have some fond memories of that one child graduating high school, and the others getting off of probation. I will also never forget the ones who put their complete trust and faith in me, and I only seemed to let them down. Whether I was laid off from the job, or fired, or whether I just didn't manage to find the right time that day to call them when they needed it. There will always be another child, but what of the ones I've lost? How do I forget the ones that got away? They were just as important as everybody else. Sure, that one 16 year old boy may have already spent years committing crimes, and being involved in the justice system by the time I got to work with him, but I wanted to bring about change. Change that was unable to come after he was arrested once again during my first week getting to know the family.

Whether I worked for a child for a day, or for a year, that initial introduction was all I needed to become emotional involved. All It took was one crying mother, or dedicated grandfather, to earn my loyalty and dedication to them in a day. But how long is it going to take to put out of memory those who quickly faded away? Those who appeared to leave me in failure. Will he be the next 17 year old in the adult county jail? Will she be the next one to have her first child at age 14? What could I have done differently? What else could have been said? What else could have been accomplished?

63

Blaming the system:

It's the easiest thing to do, blaming the system. The judge was unfair, the teacher was unfair, heck, the social service agency supervisor was unfair. We often want concrete answers to abstract problems. And, it becomes real easy to place the blame on someone specific, because it seems to make us feel better.

As I've stated earlier, I'm not exactly known in this field for being quiet and unassuming. I'm known for telling it like it is, fighting for what I believe in, and disagreeing with others when I feel they are wrong. Now, may I go too far once in a while? Absolutely. Like the time I told human resources that my boss was a moron, and has no idea what she is doing, so can somebody do something about it. Yeah, it was an interesting 89 days of employment at that agency.

But what about the bigger picture? What about your local community, city, state and government? It seems like every year I've been in this field, an agency has laid off employees, budgets have been cut, and funding has been harder to come by. Now, I fully understand that, especially in today's society, many fields of work are going through the same thing. But I am talking about people's lives here. I'm talking, not about the lives of the people who are losing their jobs and their families, but the lives of the people we were hired to help in the first place.

One of the most awkward conversations I have had with children and families were the ones in which I tried to explain why I was no longer going to be working with them much longer. You try not to tell them specifically that you are quitting a job, being laid off from a job, or being fired. Probably not best to tell a family you were fired.

I spoke earlier in my story about being laid off with a month's notice and being the last employee standing, based on my seniority. Well, what I didn't mention was that I was currently working with about 20 families at the time. That's 20 single parents, grandparents, and children, who were receiving support in improving their lives, and now it is over. That's 20 sets of teachers, counselors, neighbors and friends who supported my work with a family they cared about, and gave me their spare time and undivided attention to talk about their needs. What ever happened to them? Did they ever wonder what happened to me? Did they blame me for any future failure? Do they wonder why I never spoke to them again? There's no big goodbye, no ceremony, no transferring over to the next employee at the next agency, which is always hard on a family anyway to start over with someone else, it was just over, in what seems like an instant. And just as Ernest the unemployed is off to start a new life, those families are off by themselves, back where they started. So what now?

The resiliency of our youth

    As much as many of us in social services would like to think, we may not truly be as vitally important to our families' success as we think we are. Remember, it's not about defining success, and defining ourselves in how good we are at our jobs by checking a family success rate like they are some kind of stock on wall street. This job is not only teaching as you go along, it's about learning as you go along. And one big thing I learned is that kids are stronger then I could have ever imagined.

    In today's society, the economy is a mess, unemployment is high, and the education system is a joke. I remember, as a child, being in a classroom of about 20+ children, and thinking it was crowded. That's nothing nowadays. You're lucky if your child today is not sharing a room with over 40. Nowadays, it seems like every school is giving more days off for holidays, more 'teacher planning days' where students are off, and more half days throughout the entire school year. How much learning is really going on here?

    But through it all, these young men and women survive. Maybe that's how we should all define success. Success in life can be found simply by being able to survive. Surviving what life has to offer. Surviving what is constantly being thrown at us.

    Trust me, you haven't seen resiliency until you've seen a 10 year old girl physically drag her three younger brothers to school, crying, kicking and screaming all the way, to ensure that they receive an education, keep the family off the radar of the Department and Children and Family Services for missing too many days of school, and not become just another statistic of uneducated youth.

    I've seen a child, living in a home that's looks as

though it should be included in an episode of extreme makeover home edition, win a poetry contest. Oh, did I forget to mention that it was a contest for anyone, youth and adults, and he was only 14.

I had the pleasure of seeing one 17 year old young woman, despite having something done to her as a child that no girl, young or old, should ever have to go through, learn to become a leader. A leader in her family, a leader in her school, and a leader in her community.

If the children are our future, then the future for us will be strong. These children are battle tested, and life tested. They have knowledge beyond their years, and they truly have the resilience of a mature adult. In this day and age, they have seen it all, they have heard it all, and they have been through it all. Despite all of this, many continue through it all, hoping for the best, while expecting the least. Their confidence has been shaken, but not their resolve. There will always be that defiant teenager who seems to want to grow up too fast, and party like there is no tomorrow. However, there will also be that child who sees what many adults do not. They will see that it is not over yet. There is still time to succeed. When that time comes, they will be ready. It is not just a catchphrase. Nowadays, they really are 'born ready'.

When teaching our youth today, I think resiliency is one of the things we can leave out. The key is to help these youth harness their resilience, gain strength from it, and utilize it to succeed.

If I could do it all over again

Years ago, I was at a fast food place with a friend, picking up our food. The girl at the drive through appeared to have a sad, angry, and frustrated look on her face while placing the order, and handing us our food. As we drove off, my friend who was in the car with me, made a statement I will never forget. She simply stated, "What's up with her attitude? I never asked her to work there". I've always thought about that as I entered into the adult world of employment. I always thought to myself, well, you can't ever truly complain about what you do, because nobody asked you to do it in the first place. Of course, I certainly argued a lot with others, went against all authority, and demanded more from those in charge, but I would like to think that I was doing it 'in the best interest of the family'. Because it is, and has always been, the family that brought us there in the first place. I feel like many in social services forget that at times. They forget that all their experience, all their education, and all their licenses and degrees, are to have been obtained in order to best help others. That is what I would like to think that I have been doing with my life all these years. Helping others. What I also did not realize is that, I have not only been helping others, but also helping myself. I will forever remember my experiences in the world of social services and nonprofit. Because it is these experiences that make me who I am today. Who I am today is a man. A man who understands struggle. A man who understands the fight for equality. A Man who understands that, an unsuccessful, unsupported youth, can become an unsuccessful unsupported adult.

So I ask you this. When's the last time you saw a homeless person talking to themselves on the street? Did you give them a few bucks? If so, what would it take for you to offer such generosity and support to those who are currently on the verge of being just as unfortunate, our struggling youth? Our youth appear to be growing up faster every day, but without guidance, they are simply growing older, not wiser. And they haven't had a chance to see what I have seen in them. They haven't seen the bright future that I picture for each and every one of them.

So, in that I ask myself. What would I change about the past decade of my life. I would change nothing. What's done is done. My accomplishments, failures, my hardships, and my triumphs will always be remembered just as they are.

Many of the names and faces of the children and families I have worked with have become harder to remember these days. Like many would think, I have an easy time remembering the one's deemed 'successful'. Although, like many poker players will tell you. You can also never forget the biggest 'losses". I will always think about what could have been done differently. What resources could have been utilized? What additional support could have made all the difference. But no matter what, I can always tell myself this. At least I tried. Nobody asked me to work with these children. Nobody asked for my help. But I tried. I tried to make a difference. I tried to help.

My future

So what of my future? Well, the one last thing I forgot to mention is that, 10 years later, I find myself right back where I started. You see, the week before I started writing this book, I was laid off...again. Once again, without notice, I have left my families behind. I left that hard working educational consultant, that hardworking teacher, and that dedicated therapist behind. Once again, I put everything I was working on behind. All the goals, strategies, and interventions to be worked on, will be worked on with the family by someone else. I was only but a part of the possible solution to their troubles, but I feel hurt having to watch them see that part be taken away from them. As I've said earlier, it takes a village. I was a part of their village. I only wanted success for them. Yet all I have now given them, once again, is abandonment. So I ask myself, who am I fighting for? What am I fighting for? Why am I fighting for it in the first place?

I now wake up every morning, not feeling pressure, or fear, but feeling free. We remain in the middle of a down economy, unemployment remains an issue, but I feel free. I feel free because the only person I'm truly responsible for at the moment is me. My decisions are my own. My decisions only impact me, and my own family. I control my own destiny. Now the only question is, how do I even begin to define my own success from this point forward?

Should I continue my path towards helping others? If so, should I continue to do it 'on the front lines' or shall I seek a different path of service to this community? Throughout my childhood, right up until college graduation, I envisioned total and absolute success for myself. I saw plenty of money, nice cars, and a big house. I always dreamed of the day I would help my own family. But that was before I began my journey towards helping others not so fortunate. I'm not a child anymore. I have spent my entire adult life learning. Learning from my experience, and learning from my mistakes. Maybe I should treat myself like I treat the children I have always worked with. In this situation, I would probably tell them, "are you happy with where you are going"? If not, what can you do to get to where you want to be? What would it take for you to accomplish all of your goals? Who can help you on this journey.

Sometimes, I feel like I have no answers at this point in my life. After years of finding answers for others, I'm at a loss to solve my own questions. Maybe I feel lost once again. Only this time, I'm lost because I have nobody to help find. I've spent so much time trying to help others find their dream, I forgot to always work towards finding my own.

I would often convince myself that, no matter what I was going through, it wasn't as bad as those I was helping. Now, there are no comparisons. There is only me. My wife is obviously my partner for life, and there will now and always will be a 'we' to all statements about where to go. But, in my mind, it will always come down to me. If I can't help myself, how can I even begin to help others.

This has been my life long struggle. During my 'work week', I spent many a day contemplating the next move of others. During my 'off hours', I was kept up at night, worried about the next move of others. Throughout my journey through life, I have spent many a night contemplating my next move.

Maybe it's time I move on. Maybe it's time I found a new success. One that is not defined by the courts, the state, or the school system. I want the chance to determine my own achievements, through meeting my own goals, based upon my own efforts, and based upon my own personal and emotional triumphs.

If I were to stop judging my efforts so harshly, I would see that I have accomplished a lot in my life, and in the lives of others. I have contributed to society. I have given my all, in the best interest of others, and watched as others shined.

It's true that you don't need riches to be happy. It's also true that you don't have to struggle to find inner peace. I think it's time my next battle be with myself. No more fighting with authority. Time for me to be the authority. Time for me to shine. I'll never forget the times I interviewed for supervisory positions. When it came down to the question of, why do you feel you are best for the position, I usually said the same thing. My theory has always been, that if I am given a list of 20 families, then it will be 20 families that I try to help. However, if I am supervising 5 staff, who have 20 families each, then I am now trying to help 100 families. Seeing as how I have always worked hard to challenge myself, this seemed like the most logical choice for me as far as my goals in this profession. That challenge to help more and more is what motivated me all along.

If success is what I craved, then maybe it was more of it that I wanted. Not success for myself, but success for others. In my work life, just as in my personal life, all I really seem to want is for others to be happy. I want everyone to feel joy. I want everyone to feel what I feel, in my writing, in my comedy, and in my time spent with loved ones. Can I produce such happiness in others doing something completely different with my life. Have I finally accomplished what I was sent out to do in regards to helping children? Is everything I have done up to this point enough? Enough to ease my mind. Enough to settle for what has been achieved, and move on. Have I really succeeded already?

Perhaps, without really knowing it until now, I already found my success. Perhaps my own success has already been determined, based upon my own resiliency, my own strengths, and my own will to fight for success in others. Win or lose, what's important is how you played the game. I feel like I've had one heck of a career. But in life, a decade is but a season. I'm not retiring, I'm just leaving the field of play. I'm leaving because I've already won. I've won because I accept my own success. All I've ever wanted was success. I just didn't realize that helping others, and most importantly myself, was all I ever really needed to do to achieve it.

Made in the USA
Coppell, TX
15 March 2022

75026973R00046